NORLA
NORWEGIAN LITERATURE ABROAD

Enchanted Lion Books gratefully acknowledges the support
of NORLA for the translation and publication of this book.

LITTLE PARSLEY

ILLUSTRATED

BY

PAUL RENÉ GAUGUIN

Little Parsley

By Inger Hagerup

Translated from the Norwegian by Becky Lynn Crook

ENCHANTED LION BOOKS
NEW YORK

MISTER COCKROACH

Mister Cockroach
coat to his toes
and wearing boat-like shoes
went to the fair
and won a pair
of mini boots, size 2.

Mister Cockroach
said "Thank you so much!"
and eagerly boxed up the set.
Without further ado
he dashed home with the shoes
to flaunt for his kids and Roachette.

GUMPTIOUS, SCRUMPTIOUS

Gumptious, scrumptious gooseberry,
you who are so plump and dear,
why do you grow, year after year,
on such an angry briar?
Next spring, couldn't you instead
please hop upon an apple tree,
to grow gold and ripen there,
and let yourself get picked
without me getting pricked?

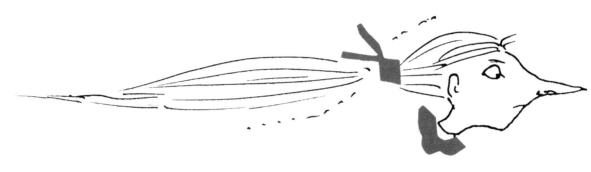

LITTLE MISS NOSEYPANTS

Little Miss Noseypants
would you like to visit France
and meet someone refined?
We are headed that way too
but we've got no space for you
so you must run behind.

THE HOUSE CALLED "NEVER-COME-BACK"

The house called "Never-Come-Back"
and the house called "Welcome-Again"
are both the very same age
and live in the very same glen.

"Never-Come-Back" has a guard dog
that growls at all who pass by.
"Welcome-Again" has a dainty cat
wearing a pale blue bow tie.

"Never-Come-Back" has a booby trap
to keep you away from its wall.
"Welcome-Again" has a tiny bell
that jingles when folks come to call.

And everyone's cheerful and happy
at the house called "Welcome-Again,"
but next door at poor "Never-Come-Back,"
there's not even the ghost of a friend.

MY UNCLE FILLS PILLS

My Uncle fills pills
at the city pharmacy.
He's slim and grim and pale and frail
and fills the powdered pills.

My Aunt bakes buttered cakes
at the city bakery when it's sunny.
She is so round and red and funny,
baking yummy, crumbly cakes.

My Cousin wrangles reptiles
for the city fire station.
It is a marvelous vocation,
wrangling writhing reptiles.

But my little niece Patrice,
who is permitted to run wild—
she is a beastly child.

SWEET PEA

I believe I was meant to be a butterfly
because I have wings—almost!
And yet I'm attached by a stem to myself.
It's really quite pleasing, you know,
to be both a flower and bird,
in praise of the day and afloat on the breeze
but on top of all that, to secretly sit
with a belly full of small peas.

THE PIG

In his pig pen stands the pig,
pondering matters important and big.

*Have the daily pork rates
grown smaller or big?*
wonders the pig.

THE CRAB

It's all very well to live in the sea
for those who can swim and splash and be free.
But those, like the crab,
stuck on the sea floor
ever to scuttle and brood,
who never can be a fish or a bird
are often in a bad mood.

WILD CHERVIL

Am I a flower?
I do not know.
I lift my parasol for show
between geraniums and vetch
and bugleweeds and pennycress.

I show up late. But in my hour,
I line the country roads and slopes
with tiny, pale-white-June-day hopes,
and then I am *summer*, and not a flower.

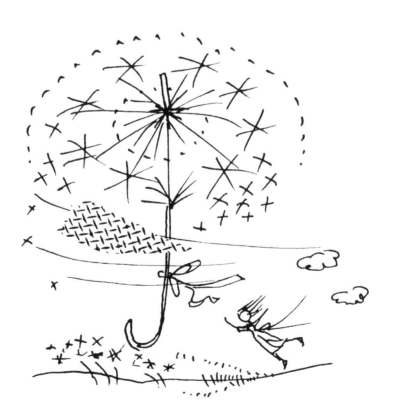

THE WASP

In a striped bathing-suit,
blazing and resolute,
he zooms with spear risen
in a bedlam of bizz'n.

A painful, poisonous prick,
a momentary blink
of rage in the clover.
And then it's all over.

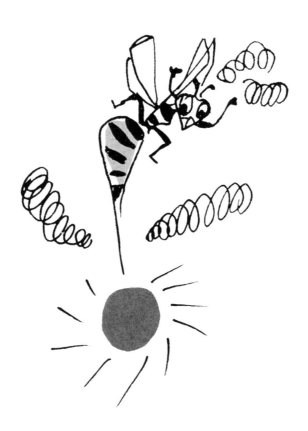

ONE IS QUITE LANKY

One is quite lanky
and Three is quite fat.
Five's feeling cranky,
Four's blind as a bat.
Two basks in her beauty, bragging.
Eight likes to tumble
and Nine is real zany.
Six likes to grumble
because he's so brainy.
And Seven is always unflagging.

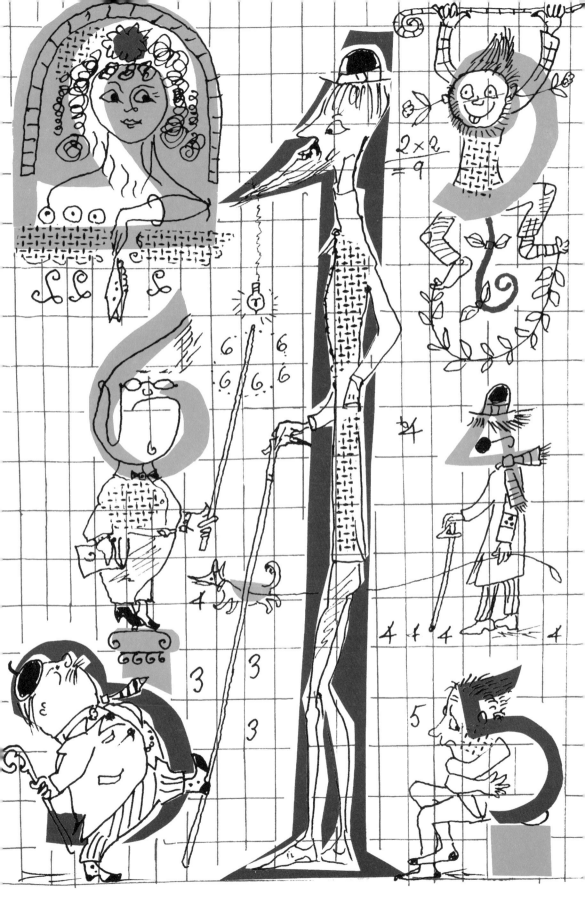

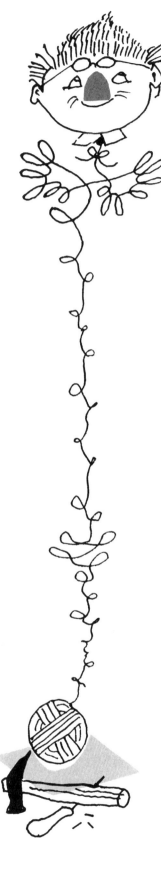

SHOEMAKER MADSEN

Shoemaker Madsen
from Bornebu
is tired of those
who complain of holes
and dearly want new shoes.
He plugs up their soles
though making lace
at a slow pace
is what he'd most like to do.
Shoemaker Madsen
from Bornebu.

PENNALINA PENNALINK

Pennalina, pennalink
dips her pensive head in ink
so we can read her prose
of a's and b's and c's and *whoops!*
scribbled down in curlicues
with her pointy nose.

THE HEDGEHOG

Bristling is what the small hedgehog does best
whenever he's feeling afraid.
Up goes his prickly pincushion of fright
to warn all intruders away.

It's no more than a bluster of tough,
for he's truly devoted to peace.
Before long, he lowers his burlapy thistles,
hoping that nobody sees.

THEY CALL ME RADICCHIO

They call me Radicchio
but I'm really a troll, so you know.
Thick-tummied, purplish-green,
a lowbred, earthy fiend.

There's nothing like growing stout
and pushing my belly out,
while squatting in the radicchi row,
a bitter Trolldicchio.

ROBIN REDBREAST

No one wears lighter tail feathers,
or has such a silky shirt on.
And no one can be so suddenly close
and then be so suddenly gone.

Alight on a plump twig for a small nap
and keep watch with a cheerful eye:
Humans are really such harmless saps
for they—fortunately—cannot fly!

LITTLE PARSLEY

Little Parsley in the garden bed,
pale green dress and ruffly head.
Why so still,
Little Parsley, dear?
Are you hoping
to go to the ball this year?

First English-language edition published in 2019 by Enchanted Lion Books
67 West Street, 317A, Brooklyn, NY 11222
Originally published in Norwegian in 1961 as *Lille persille*
Copyright © 1961 by H. Aschehoug & Co. (W. Nygaard) AS
Published by agreement with Oslo Literary Agency
Copyright © 2019 for the English-language edition by Enchanted Lion Books
Translation Copyright © 2019 by Enchanted Lion Books
Production & layout: Julie Kwon
All rights reserved under International and Pan-American Copyright Conventions
A CIP record is on file with the Library of Congress
ISBN: 978-1-59270-286-2
Printed in China by R. R. Donnelley Asia Printing Solutions, Ltd.

First Printing

Inger Hagerup (1905-1985) made her literary debut in 1939 with the poetry collection *I Got Lost in the Woods*. Her later poems for children are classics in Norwegian children's literature. Hagerup also composed radio plays and reinterpreted Shakespeare and Goethe. She published multiple memoirs in the 1960's. Above all a poet of love, Hagerup's poetry also touches on themes of nature, death, and feminism and was greatly influenced by her involvement in the Norwegian resistance against the Nazis during World War II.

Paul René Gauguin (1911-1976) was born in Cophenhagen, the son of Pola Gauguin and the grandson of the French post-impressionist Paul Gauguin. A painter, sculptor, set designer, and illustrator, he is well remembered for his innovative color woodcuts. He first learned wood cutting techniques while on fishing trips in Ibiza and Mallorca. His art draws inspiration from Max Ernst, Vincent van Gogh, and Georges Braque.

Becky Lynn Crook is a writer and literary translator. In 2010, she founded *SAND*, an English literary journal in Berlin. She began translating literature while living in the Netherlands. Her translations have appeared in *Granta*, *Guernica*, and *Freeman's*, and she is working on writing her own first novel. After coming across Inger Hagreup's children's poems in 2011, she was inspired to introduce the poems to international readers. She currently lives on Bainbridge Island, Washington with her husband, daughter, and cat, Momo.